STUDENT

6

Discipleship Lessons

Friends of JESUS

Published by: Mesoamerica Region Discipleship Ministries

www.SdmiResources.MesoamericaRegion.org

Copyright © 2019 - All rights reserved

ISBN: 978-1-63580-120-0

All of the scripture verses quoted are from the NIV Bible.

Translated into English from Spanish by: Bethany Cyr

Printed in the United States

# BE A FRIEND OF JESUS

"But when the set time had fully come, God sent his Son, born of a woman, born under the law, to redeem those under the law, that we might receive adoption to sonship".
*Galatians 4:4-5*

The angel Gabriel, sent by God, appeared to a virgin named Mary and told her that she would give birth to a baby boy. She was to name her son Jesus; he would be great and would be called the Son of God, and he would save the world from their sins.

A census was being done, so Mary and her husband Joseph had to travel to Bethlehem near the time the baby was expected to be born. "While they were there, the time came for the baby to be born, and she gave birth to her firstborn, a son. She wrapped him in cloths and placed him in a manger, because there was no guest room available for them."

(Taken from Luke 1:26-35 and 2:1-7)

# To become a friend of Jesus:

Write one of these words on each line to complete the phrase.

Ask , Begin, Accept, Believe, Know, Tell

**1.** _____ God that you have disobeyed him.

**2.** _____ that God loves you.

**3.** _____ that God sent His son, Jesus, so that you can be forgiven.

**4.** _____ for and receive God's forgiveness.

**5.** _____ that Jesus is your savior and best friend.

**6.** _____ to live as a child of God.

3

# To Become a Best Friend:

Write a word on each line to complete the sentence. The letters, are arranged backwards.

**1** _____ more about God. Read and memorize verses from the Bible.

(nraeL)

**2** _____ with God. Thank him for Jesus. Ask him to help you be obedient and do the right thing.

(klaT)

**3** _____ others about God's love.

(lleT)

**4** _____ with other Christians.

(teeM)

**5** _____ God to forgive you if you disobey. Then you will continue to live as Jesus' friend.

(ksA)

4

# Alphabet Soup

Look for 4 hidden words and use them to make a sentence.

| C | S | C | O | M | E | S | O | S | S |
|---|---|---|---|---|---|---|---|---|---|
| N | A | N | E | J | J | A | F | A | H |
| A | J | M | O | U | A | R | L | Z | H |
| G | G | A | I | K | R | V | Z | H | L |
| O | V | T | M | N | A | A | I | L | F |
| D | R | J | A | T | A | B | O | A | R |
| D | O | S | I | I | A | E | R | A | O |
| Y | O | O | R | A | E | T | A | G | M |
| E | N | C | P | O | O | E | R | R | B |

Sentence:

5

# 2 IT'S GOOD TO BE FRIENDS WITH JESUS!

Zacchaeus did not obey God. He took too much tax money from people.

One day Zacchaeus met Jesus. Jesus loved Zacchaeus. Jesus wanted to help him change.

Zacchaeus became Jesus' friend. He was sorry he had done bad things. He wanted to obey God.

Zacchaeus said: "I will return the money I took and give money to help the poor."

"Today God has forgiven you," Jesus told him.

(Taken from Luke 19:1-10)

# CROSSWORD

Solve the following crossword puzzle using the key words from the story of **Zaccheus**.

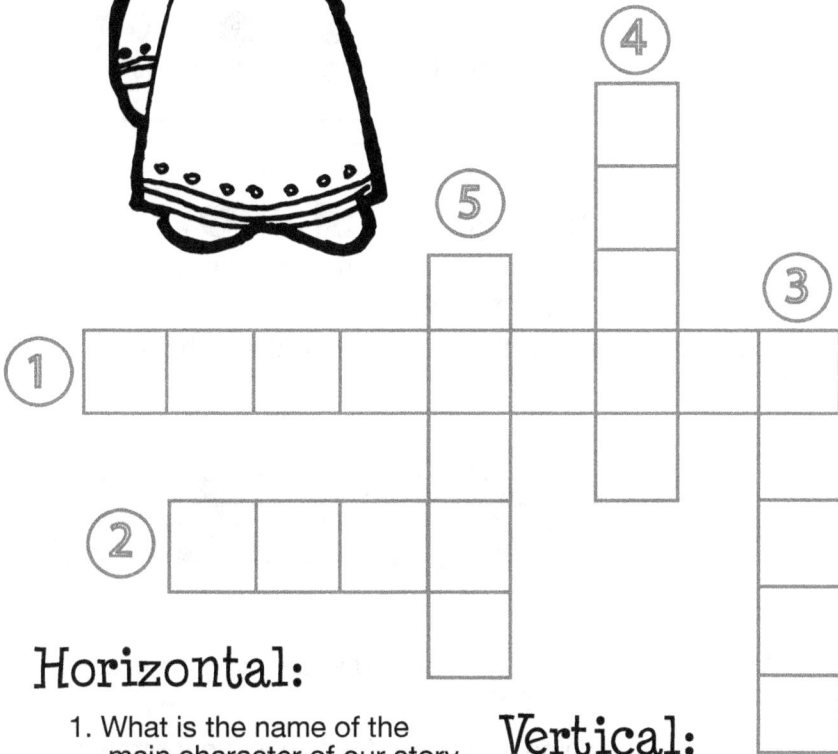

## Horizontal:

1. What is the name of the main character of our story.

2. To whom did he give half of his possessions?

## Vertical:

3. How did Zaccheus feel after he talked with Jesus.

4. What did Zaccheus return?

5. What characteristic is used to describe Zaccheus?

# Discover the WORD

Below the lines are symbols. On each line write the letter that goes with the symbol.

| ❀ | ✑ | ✓ | ✗ | ✐ | † | ☆ | ✄ | ☎ | ▼ |
|---|---|---|---|---|---|---|---|---|---|
| A | E | F | G | H | I | K | L | M | N |
| ✈ | ✉ | ✿ | ▲ | ❄ | ● | ✪ | ✚ | ■ | |
| O | P | R | S | T | U | V | W | Y | |

1 God is always ____________ . God is
✚ † ❄ ✐ ■ ✈ ●

____________ when good things
✚ † ❄ ✐ ■ ✈ ●

happen. He is also with you when bad things happen. He can help you.

"God is our protection and our strength. He always helps in times of trouble."
*Psalms 46:1 (ICB)*

2 You can ____________ to God at any time. You can
❄ ❀ ✄ ☆

tell God everything you need. God hears your prayers.

"I call on you, my God, for you will answer me; turn your ear to me and hear my prayer."
*Psalms 17:6*

**3** God _____  you to obey him. He even

helps you to ✚ ❀ ▼ ❄️ _____ to obey him.

> "... for it is God who works in you to will and to act in order to fulfill his good purpose." *Pilippians 2:13*

**4** God is sad if you disobey him. But he will

 ✓ ✈ ❀ ✗ ✝ ✹ ↝ _____ you if you ask him.

> "If we confess our sins, he is faithful and just and will forgive us our sins ..." *1 John 1:9*

**5** God is preparing a special _____ for you in

heaven. You will go to live with God when you die.

# FIND THE TREASURE

**3**

> "Jesus answered, 'It is written: Man shall not live on bread alone, but on every word that comes from the mouth of God.'"
> *Matthew 4:4*

There are many ways to find the treasures that God has for us. There are two ways that are very easy and we can all use them.

Matthew 4:4 teaches us that, while food is important, it is not the only thing we need to live. The Word of God (the Bible) and prayer are very important if we want to grow in our spiritual life.

In Matthew 6:9-13, Jesus taught his disciples a model prayer so that his followers would understand what communication with God should be like.

# Questions & Answers

One way to get to know Jesus better is by reading the Bible. The Bible is God's message to us. In 2 Timothy 3:16-17 we are told why the Bible is important to Christians. Read the passage and then join with a line the question with the corresponding answer.

**1** Who gave us the Bible?

**2** What does the Bible teach us?

**3** Why is the Bible important?

**A** It helps us know Jesus better.

**B** God

**C** What is right and wrong.

# Draw and Pray

Jesus told us some things that we can pray for. Can you think of something you can pray for? Remember that you can pray at any time and anywhere.

Draw or outline your hand in the space below. Write something you want to pray for on each finger. In the center of the hand write, "Thank you, God." Put your drawing somewhere in your house where you can see it and be reminded to pray.

Backward Words

# Backwards Words

Learn the Lord's Prayer. Complete the Lord's Prayer by reversing the letters of the words that are below the lines. Write the correct words on the lines. Try to memorize this prayer. Say it over and over so you can remember it.

"Our _____ in heaven,
(rehtaF)

hallowed be your name.

Your kingdon _____,
(emoc)

Your will be done,

on _____ as it is in heaven.
(htrae)

Give _____ today our daily bread.
(su)

And forgive us our _____,
(stbed)

as we also have forgiven our debtors.

And lead us not into _____,
(noitatpmet)

but deliver us from the _____ one."
(live)

Matthew 6:9-13

# LEARNING TO PLEASE JESUS

"... give thanks in all circumstances; for this is God's will for you in Christ Jesus"
*1 Thessalonians 5:18*

One day, Jesus was preaching to a large group of people. After he had been there for some time, the disciples came to Jesus and told him that there were alot of people, and they were begining to get hungry. Jesus asked them to see if anyone had any food.

The disciples searched and returned to tell Jesus that one boy had 2 fish and 5 loaves of bread. Jesus took the fish and the bread, thanked God for it, and gave it to the disciples to give to the people. All of the people had food to eat and there was even some left over.

Taken from
John 6:1-15.

# A Boy and His Lunch

Color the picture of the boy giving his lunch to Jesus.

# Circle of Friendship

Follow the path to the center of the circle. Don't cross any lines.
When you reach the center, you'll find your best friend, Jesus.

START

# SECRET CODE

Jesus wants us to love others. Use the words in the box to complete the verse.

A friend _____ you _____ the
☆          △
time. A brother is _____ there
◯
to _____ you.
▢

_____ 17:17 (ICB)

▢ help
◇ Proverbs
△ all
◯ always
☆ loves

# 5

## WELL DONE!

Jesus was in the desert to pray and spend time with God. He did not eat for 40 days. Satan went and tempted Jesus. Satan tried to make Jesus go against God's commands.

Each time that Jesus was tempted, he chose to do good instead. He used verses from God's Word to make Satan go away.

Taken from Luke 4:1-13.

God wants to help us do good things. Use these recommendations to help you stay away from temptation.

# 5 Fingers

Draw along the dotted line to complete the hand. Explain what is written in each finger.

Stay away from people, places and things that make you want to do bad things.

Tell Satan to go away. Remember, Jesus ordered Satan to go away.

Ask other Christians to help you.

Ask God to help you to make good choices.

Know what Jesus wants you to do.

# Jesus was tempted...

Satan tempted Jesus to turn stones into bread. What did Jesus say to Satan?

Read Matthew 4:4 in your Bible and find the answer.

_____

_____

_____

_____

**2**

Satan tempted Jesus to jump from the temple and let the angels rescue him. What did Jesus say to Satan?

Read Matthew 4:7 in your Bible and find the answer..

_____

_____

_____

_____

_____

**3**

The devil tempted Jesus a final time. He told Jesus that he could rule all nations if he bowed down and worshiped him. What did Jesus say to Satan?

Read Matthew 4:10 in your Bible and find the answer.

_____

_____

# How Can I Serve?

Put an **X** in the box next to the activities that you already do and put an **O** next to the ones you still need to do.

1. Go to church often. Christians in the church will help you grow as Jesus' friend. You will be able to care for and help others live for God.

2. Give money to God. When you put money in the offering at your church, your church uses the money to help others learn about Jesus and for other good things.

3. Tell other people how God has helped you. This will help others to believe in God.

4. Help out when your church has a special project to do. Work is faster when many people do it together.

5. Invite your friends and your family to church. Then they will get to hear about Jesus.

Can you think of other ways that you can serve in the church? Write them here:

_____

_____

_____

_____

# 6 THE SUPER TEAM

"Therefore, as we have opportunity, let us do good to all people, especially to those who belong to the family of believers."

*Galatians 6:10*

In this passage, the apostle explains that your relationships with others are very important. He said that if we know a little more than someone else, we should help them. We must help each other. We should never think ourselves as better than others. That is why we should not compare ourselves to others.

We should always spend our time doing good things. This will allow us to become better people. The Bible says, "Therefore, as we have opportunity, let us do good to all people, especially to those who belong to the family of believers."

Gal. 6:1-6

When you become a Christian, you also become a Child of God and Jesus' friend . Christians follow God and the church. Here are 4 ways that the church can help you grow. Under the blank spaces you will see a number and a symbol. On the table, find where the number and the symbol meet and that is the letter you need. Write the letters on the lines to complete the sentences.

| | 1 | 2 | 3 | 4 | 5 | 6 |
|---|---|---|---|---|---|---|
| ⊕ | V | E | Y | O | J | D |
| ⊖ | X | W | U | I | H | L |
| ⊛ | K | P | G | N | R | F |
| ⊘ | C | S | A | M | B | T |

# Fellowship

In your church you can enjoy fellowship. Fellowship is when

_____ enjoy doing things together.
⊛6  ⊛5  ⊖4  ⊕2  ⊛4  ⊕6  ⊘2

Christians have _____
⊛6  ⊕2  ⊖6  ⊖6  ⊕4  ⊖2  ⊘2  ⊖5  ⊖4  ⊛2

when they read the Bible, pray and praise God together. They also have fellowship when they have fun or work on special projects

_____ .
⊘6  ⊕4  ⊛3  ⊕2  ⊘6  ⊖5  ⊕2  ⊛5

23

# Bible Study

The church helps you study the Bible. In the church, you learn about the Bible. Your Sunday school teacher and your pastor

_____ what the Bible _____.

⊘6  ⊕2  ⊘3  ⊘1  ⊖5          ⊘2  ⊘3  ⊕3  ⊘2

They also teach you how to put into practice the things you learn.

# Praise

Praise is how we let God know how much we love, honor and respect him. You can praise God by yourself. But it is also important to praise him with your church. There are lots of ways that you can praise Jesus with your friends. You can

_____

⊘2  ⊖4  ⊗4  ⊗3          ⊘2  ⊕4  ⊗4  ⊗3  ⊘2

of praise to God. You can _____ to God. You

⊗2  ⊗5  ⊘3  ⊕3

can _____ others how God has helped you.

⊘6  ⊕2  ⊖6  ⊖6

And you can tell them about your _____ for Jesus.

⊖6  ⊕4  ⊕1  ⊕2

# Help Others

God wants us to help each other in the church. Tell your church

friends when you are _____. Tell them when you

⊘2  ⊖4  ⊘1  ⊗1

are having problems. Ask them to _____ for you.

⊗2  ⊗5  ⊘3  ⊕3

# Time with God

Look in the Bible for the following verses. Look at what the Bible says about living as children of God and friends of Jesus. Practice repeating Galatians 6:10. Think of ways you can help others.

**1**   Acts 4:32-35

_____

**2**   Acts 12:1-5

_____

**3**   Acts 17:10-12

_____

**4**   Romans 12 :10-16

_____

**5**   Galatians 6:10

_____

**6**   Ephesians 4:29 - 5:2

_____

**7**   Colossians 3: 12-14

_____

# Friends of Jesus

# Certificate of Recognition

Presented to:

_____

for having completed the Basic Bible Study
course for children, "Friends of Jesus"!

_____
Discipler's Signature

_____
Pastor's Signature

_____
Date

www.ingramcontent.com/pod-product-compliance
Lightning Source LLC
Chambersburg PA
CBHW060606030426
42337CB00019B/3630